Discipleship
ESSENTIALS

Disciple Making Essentials Series

Ken Adams

Discipleship
ESSENTIALS

ImpactDisciples.com

BEFORE YOU BEGIN...

Jesus Christ told us to *"make disciples of all nations."* If we are going to be successful in doing so, we need to know what a disciple looks like. We need to have a clear definition of a disciple. This definition needs to come from Christ. The original disciple maker is the one who defines a disciple.

Discipleship Essentials is a course designed to help you understand the definition of a disciple. As you work through these weekly lessons, remember that the truths discovered in these lessons will serve as a guide for what a disciple looks like and whether or not you are becoming one. The biblical principles you will learn in this course will give you a foundation for understanding disciple making for years to come.

In order to lay a solid foundation, I would like to recommend a few things. *First,* give your best to each lesson. Don't rush through the lessons and skim the reading. Give it your best effort and look up all the verses so that you know what God is saying. *Second,* commit yourself to the daily scripture reading. The scripture reading is designed to supplement the lesson and using the acrostic **A.C.T.S.** will help God's Word come alive to you every day. *Third,* commit yourself to the weekly memory verse. Memorizing scripture is one of the most important things you can do to grow spiritually, so give this discipline your best effort. *Fourth,* be present at the group meetings. Anyone can do the lessons on his or her own, but you can't discuss what you are learning on your own. The group time is a valuable aspect of your spiritual growth process.

Over the next few weeks, I pray that you will discover some of the essential marks of a disciple, and I pray that these essentials will be true of you for a lifetime.

Being and Building Disciples,

Ken Adams

WEEK ONE:
DEFINING A DISCIPLE

Goal: To understand what a disciple of Christ looks like.

Let's begin with a question. Write your definition of what a disciple of Jesus Christ is? _____
_____
_____

I ask you that question because someone once asked it of me. I had just finished teaching a group of pastors about the subject of discipleship when a man asked me what I thought a disciple of Jesus looked like. To be honest, I think he was testing me more than truly asking for a definition. I think he had his definition, and I think he wanted to see if mine matched his. It didn't!

I told this fellow that a disciple of Jesus is someone who is looking more like Jesus. In other words, a disciple is someone who is in a process of spiritual development. They never arrive or graduate; they simply continue developing. Over time, a disciple looks more like Jesus and not less like Jesus. Look at how Jesus said it Himself in Luke 6:40? _____
_____
_____

A disciple that looks like his teacher is one that lives like his teacher and leads like his teacher. A disciple of Jesus lives and leads like Jesus!

THE DISCIPLE TEST

The best way to define a disciple is to see what traits are consistently passed down from one disciple to the next. In other words, the disciples of Jesus would have some of the same traits that Jesus had. A disciple of a disciple of Jesus would have some of the same traits of Jesus as well. If disciples of Christ kept making more disciples of Christ, pretty soon you would have a whole

MEMORY VERSE

Luke 6:40

WEEKLY BIBLE READING

Read the passage and write out an insight on at least one of the following:

A: Attitude to change
C: Command to obey
T: Truth to believe
S: Sin to confess

☐ **MONDAY**
Mark 3:13-21

1

world of people looking more and more like Christ. Wouldn't that be exactly what Jesus wanted?

When you look at Jesus' life and then look at His disciples and their disciples, you see a list of common traits. These traits give us a great definition of what a disciple ought to look like. If a trait is found in Jesus and that same trait is found in Jesus' disciple and found in that disciple's disciple, then it ought to be found in you and me. When you examine Jesus and His disciples and their disciples, here is some of what you find.

They all belong to the same mission and movement!
They all worship and magnify God the Father!
They are experiencing spiritual growth and maturity!
They are ministering and serving others!
They are managing their life resources for God's honor!
They are messengers of the gospel!
They are multiplying and reproducing disciples!

Take a minute and read Acts 2:42-47 and see if you can identify the traits above in that passage. All seven of them are present, and all seven can be found in Christ's life and the lives of His disciples. They all pass the test!

DISCIPLE DEFINED

It's easy to define a disciple as someone who is looking more like Jesus, but fleshing out that definition can be difficult. It might be helpful to describe a disciple with some consistent terminology. If our commission is to make disciples, then it might help if we agreed on what one looks like. Here is a diagram to help us summarize and describe the traits of a disciple. This description is not the only way to describe a disciple, but it is one way, and it can help us identify the traits that we should look for in Christ followers. See how many of them are true of you?

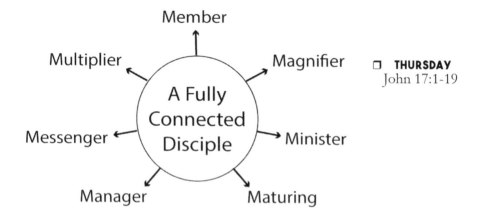

☐ **THURSDAY**
John 17:1-19

CONNECTED AND DEVELOPING

Before the original disciples met Jesus, it is safe to say they were totally disconnected from Christ and were underdeveloped spiritually. After being with Jesus for a number of years, it is safe to say that the disciples had become fully connected to Christ and were developing spiritually. Jesus' target was to connect people and develop people spiritually. This is how Jesus made disciples. How were the disciples described in Acts 4:13?

☐ **FRIDAY**
1 John 2:1-14

_____

_____

When you have been with Jesus you begin to look more like Jesus!

DISCIPLES DESCRIBED

For the next several weeks, we will be studying the traits of a disciple. The following seven traits will be the description we will use for this study. Take a few minutes to read each trait and determine which ones are true of you and which ones are not.

_____

_____

_____

_____

_____

_____

_____

_____

_____

_____

_____

_____

_____

_____

_____

_____

_____

_____

_____

_____

A disciple is a member! Disciples of Christ believe and belong together. They share truth, and they share community. This was true for the original twelve, for the Church in Jerusalem, and the Church in the other areas.

A disciple is a magnifier! Disciples of Christ magnify Christ in worship. They are committed to a lifestyle of exalting the risen Lord and pointing others to Him.

A disciple is a minister! Disciples of Christ are servants. They look to meet the needs of others and are willing to serve people in need. A disciple uses his or her spiritual gifts to minister for Christ.

A disciple is maturing! A disciple of Christ is growing spiritually. A disciple of Christ moves from infancy in the faith to adulthood in the faith. A disciple is a person who is growing in their knowledge and experience with God.

A disciple is a manager! A disciple of Christ uses his or her time, treasure, temple, and talent to honor and glorify God. A disciple knows that their resources come from God and are to be managed for His purposes.

A disciple is a messenger! Disciples of Christ talk about Christ. They are missionaries to the rest of the world.

A disciple is a multiplier! A disciple of Christ multiplies more disciples of Christ. They make disciples that make more disciples.

The goal over the next few weeks is to become more like Jesus!

QUESTIONS FOR GROUP DISCUSSION
OR PERSONAL REFLECTION

➤ Open your group with prayer and share a highlight from your week.

➤ Take a minute and share your definition you wrote at the beginning of this lesson. Are the groups' answers different or similar?

➤ How would the early disciples define a disciple?

➤ Read Luke 6:40. How does this clarify the definition of a disciple?

➤ What happens if the definition of a disciple is not clear in the church?

➤ Read Acts 4:13. What speaks to you the most about this verse?

➤ How did the traits of Jesus get passed down to the earliest church members? How does it happen today?

➤ Which of the seven traits described in this lesson are true of your life and which are not? Are you ready to grow in those areas?

➤ Take a minute to share prayer requests and pray for each other.

WEEK TWO:
A DISCIPLE IS A MEMBER

Goal: To understand the trait of membership.

The original disciples did not have a membership class and they did not have a membership process to go through, but, trust me, they were very much members of Christ's mission and movement. When Jesus asked His disciples to *"come follow Me,"* He was asking them to make a commitment. Jesus was asking His original disciples to join His mission and His movement. Being a disciple truly meant being a member.

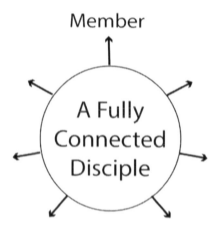

Member

A Fully Connected Disciple

MEMORY VERSE

Matthew 16:24

WEEKLY BIBLE READING

Read the passage and write out an insight on at least one of the following:

A: Attitude to change
C: Command to obey
T: Truth to believe
S: Sin to confess

☐ **MONDAY**
Matthew 16:24-28

A DISCIPLE BELIEVES AND BELONGS

Whatever terminology you choose to use, one thing is certain: the disciples "joined" Jesus' team. They became members or partners or whatever else you choose to call them. The point is, the original disciples chose to belong to Jesus and to each other.

This concept of disciples *belonging* and *believing* together makes it very clear that a disciple is a "member"! In the same way Jesus' twelve disciples joined His mission, the New Testament disciples joined His mission as well. That's exactly what church membership is: joining the

7

mission of Jesus!

WEEKLY BIBLE READING

☐ **TUESDAY**
   Acts 2:37-41

In Acts chapter two, there were three thousand people saved as a result of Peter's preaching. That meant they all *believed* the same thing. Right after they accepted Peter's message of salvation, they were all baptized and started meeting together in the temple court and in houses. That meant they all *belonged* to each other. A disciple is someone who *believes* and *belongs* to the mission and movement of Christ!

In today's church, membership means the same thing it did two thousand years ago. We might go about it differently, but when it is all said and done, being a member of a church is making a commitment to the mission and movement of Christ in a local family of believers.

Think of it this way. The church is described in the Scriptures as a flock, a bride, a body, a temple, a family, and a holy people. In every description there is the idea of commitment. Sheep are committed to the shepherd and the flock. A married couple are committed to each other and their families. Every part of my body is com-

☐ **WEDNESDAY**
   Romans 12:9-21

mitted to the head as well as every other part of my body. In the same way, the church is a movement of people committed to the same mission.

I often wonder why a disciple of Christ wouldn't want to commit to a local body of believers? It seems like the trend these days is *believe* and belong without committing. In a marriage that's called "living together." Every disciple needs to be a committed member of the mission and movement of Jesus Christ.

Have you made a commitment to belong to a local body of believers? _____

WHAT DOES MEMBERSHIP MEAN?

Being a disciple of Jesus in the New Testament days would more than likely mean that your family would have nothing to do with you. Christians in the first century were typically ostracized from their family and friends thus making membership in a local church vitally important. The church truly was a **family** in the first century.

That family of believers shared several things in common. The first mark of membership was salvation. How were members described in Acts 2:38? _____

_____

_____

❐ **THURSDAY**
1 Corinthians
12:12-26

Repentance, being forgiven, and being filled with the Holy Spirit were all indicators that members of the church were first members of God's family.

A second mark of membership was **baptism**. Water baptism by immersion was an outward symbol of an inner commitment. In the New Testament baptism was practiced in public settings not in the seclusion of a church building. When a person was baptized they were truly "going public" with their faith in Jesus. What took place in Acts 2:41? _____

_____

_____

❐ **FRIDAY**
Ephesians
4:1-16

Have you taken the step of baptism by immersion since your time of salvation? _____

The third mark of membership was **involvement**. The concept of a church membership role did not exist in the Jerusalem church. The first church had no such thing as inactive members. If you were active in the church, you were a member! If you were not active, you were not a member. Membership equaled involvement. What word describes involvement in Acts 2:42?

_____

Today we have lots of churches with more members than active participants. We have accepted the assumption that being an inactive member is acceptable to God.

9

Why would Jesus sacrifice His very life to have an inactive disciple in His church?

The last mark of a member in the church was **unified doctrine**. In the earliest days of the church, agreement on the major teachings of the faith were essential to being a member. What did Paul write in Romans 16:17? _____

_____

_____

Paul is very strong on the need for purity and unity in what is being taught in the church. Agreement in sound doctrine is clearly a requirement for being a church member.

WHERE HAS COMMITMENT GONE?

Church involvement today looks quite different from the way Christ intended it to be. Today there is a serious lack of commitment in the local church. Our consumer culture has left commitment at the door. Today many Christians jump from church to church, and in essence this weakens the mission of the church. Yes, there are times when a person needs to change churches, but it should be for the right reason. Swapping discontented sheep from one church to another is not the right reason. We must do better than that!

I want to encourage all who are doing this study to commit to a church that teaches the Bible and makes disciples. The church needs you, and you need the church! Make a commitment to belong to a local body of believers. That is what disciples do.

QUESTIONS FOR GROUP DISCUSSION
OR PERSONAL REFLECTION

☛ Open your group with prayer and share a praise for something God has done.

☛ Share one or two organizations that you "belong" to these days (besides the church) and why you have joined them.

☛ In your opinion do you think the value of church membership has changed much in your lifetime? Why or why not?

☛ Read Acts 20:28. Why should church membership be important to Christians today?

☛ Take a minute to discuss the marks of membership and how they are demonstrated or not demonstrated in your own life.

☛ How does believing and belonging help a Christian stay stronger in their faith?

☛ How does a lack of commitment to a local church hurt an individual and the entire body of Christ?

☛ Why does sheep swapping weaken and hurt the cause of Christ in the world today?

☛ Take a minute and share prayer requests and pray together.

WEEK THREE:
A DISCIPLE IS A MAGNIFIER

MEMORY VERSE

Luke 24:52

Goal: To understand the trait of worship

The first church in Jerusalem might not have had an organ, a piano, a guitar, or a drum set, but I promise you they had worship! The church in the New Testament was filled with worshippers. Look at how the church is described in Acts 2:47? _____
_____

WEEKLY BIBLE READIN

Read the passage and write out an insight on at least one of the following:

A: Attitude to change
C: Command to obey
T: Truth to believe
S: Sin to confess

A church described as a place where people are "praising God" is a church filled with magnifiers or worshippers. Being a disciple means being a magnifier!

☐ **MONDAY**
Matthew 3:13-17

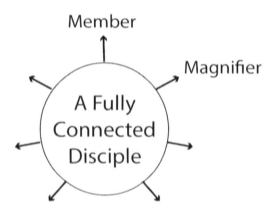

Member

Magnifier

A Fully Connected Disciple

A DISCIPLE MAGNIFIES AND GLORIFIES

Every disciple of Jesus ought to be a worshipper! If you claim to follow Jesus, you should be marked by a lifestyle of magnifying God. The original disciples pointed people to God and magnified Him in their praise and worship. They magnified and worshipped God because Jesus gave them an example of magnifying and glorifying the Father.

Even a quick reading of the Gospels will reveal to you the priority Jesus placed on magnifying the Father in His life. Jesus pointed to His Father in everything He did. In John 5:19 Jesus said, *"Truly, truly, I say to you, the Son can do nothing of his own accord, but only what he sees the Father doing. For whatever the Father does, that the Son does likewise."* In John 6:38 Jesus said, *"For I have come down from heaven, not to do my own will but the will of him who sent me."* Jesus gave the Father credit for every single thing He did on earth. That is magnifying the Lord!

In Matthew 28:9, after Jesus was resurrected from the grave, the disciples were found *"worship[ping] him."* As the Church expanded and grew, the priority of worshipping and praising Jesus only increased. Even to this day, the Church places a high priority on the worship and magnification of the Father. Throughout history the purpose of the creation has been to worship the creator!

So how is the priority of magnifying the Father fitting into your life? Is worship a consistent practice in your spiritual journey? Is your life known as one that consistently points people to God? Are you known as a regular worshipper? How consistent is the practice of worship in your life? _____

_____

True disciples are marked by a lifestyle of magnifying and exalting God. They do not worship because they "have to"; they worship because they "want to." Praise and worship to God is the natural outflow of being a disciple of Jesus Christ. When Jesus saves you from your sins and gives you new life, you just can't stop praising Him.

WHAT DOES MAGNIFYING MEAN?

When you use a magnifying glass, you make an object larger. That same concept is exactly what it means to be a disciple that magnifies Christ. A disciple makes Christ larger through praise and worship!

Magnifying Christ and making Him larger is really a lifestyle, but it demonstrates itself in two specific disciplines. Magnifiers practice private worship and public worship.

Private worship is having a regular time in your life when you meet with God and focus on Him. In doing so, you magnify the Lord and make Him the focus of your attention and your affection. Jesus modeled this when He would get away from the crowds and be alone with the Father. What do you see in Mark 1:35? _____
_____
_____

❏ **THURSDAY**
Ephesians 5:15-21

What does Psalm 91:1 say about private time with God? _____
_____
_____

Public worship is the discipline of gathering with other believers to magnify God. When disciples gather together to magnify God, it honors Him and strengthens those disciples. What does Psalm 95:6 say?_____
_____
_____

❏ **FRIDAY**
Psalm 150

Is this verse written in the singular or plural person?

What does Psalm 84:4 say?_____
_____
_____

You are blessed when you prioritize worship in your life. In Ephesians 5:19 what does Paul tell church members to do? _____
_____
_____

What does Hebrews 13:15 say? _____
_____
_____

The Bible is filled with examples of the priority of public and corporate worship. These examples should make it very clear that a trait found in disciples of Jesus is magnifying the Father. Is that trait found in you?_____

_____

WHAT HAS HAPPENED TO WORSHIP?

If a disciple is not careful, worship can be pushed to the back burner of life. Instead of making the practice of worship a priority, some have made it optional. That is never what Christ intended. Whenever this happens, it is because we have believed a lie. What does Romans 1:25 say? _____

_____

Once someone forgets who the creator is and who the creature is, the door is open for all kinds of problems. Today, many people do not make magnifying God a priority because they have forgotten who they are and who God is! Here are some problems that occur when we start worshipping the creature.

Other things become more important! When a person starts worshipping the creation instead of the creator, it changes their priorities. Instead of making worship a consistent practice, it becomes a matter of convenience. In today's culture many people are neglecting the priority of worship because other things are more important to them.

Worship becomes more about the person than God! When a person forgets who God is, they will approach worship from the standpoint of what they can get rather than what they can give. When worship is about the worshipper, their needs become all that matters. We live in a culture today where many people only worship if it makes them happy.

Personality-centered worship! When the creature becomes more important than the creator, worship will become personality centered rather than God centered. When the worshipper is more concerned about who is singing or preaching than whether or not God is being magnified, there is a problem. The lie has been bought!

QUESTIONS FOR GROUP DISCUSSION OR PERSONAL REFLECTION

➤ Open the group with prayer and share a lesson God has taught you recently.

➤ Describe the type of worship you remember as a child.

➤ In your opinion why does Satan attack the priority of worship as much as he does?

➤ Why do you think the priority of consistent worship has decreased among many believers today?

➤ How consistent are you in private worship and public worship?

➤ What would you tell someone who is having trouble connecting with God privately?

➤ Read Psalm 95:6 and Ephesians 5:19 and describe the benefits of corporate and public worship.

➤ Do you think any of the problems regarding worship mentioned in this lesson were a problem in the New Testament church? How much of a problem are these things today?

➤ Would people know you are a disciple of Christ by the priority of private and public worship in your life?

➤ Take a minute to share prayer concerns and then pray together.

WEEK FOUR:
A DISCIPLE IS A MINISTER

Goal: To understand the trait of ministry.

The word "minister" simply means to meet a need. Meeting a need is exactly what Jesus came to do. Jesus came to serve and not to be served. Jesus came to meet our need for salvation. He served us by laying down His life as a sacrifice on the cross for our sin. How does Mark 10:45 describe Jesus? _____

_____

_____

With Jesus as their model, the original disciples learned firsthand the importance of serving. Not only did Jesus serve and His disciples serve, but their disciples also served. Serving was a trait that was passed from one generation of disciples to the next. What does Acts 2:45 tell us about the church in Jerusalem? _____

_____

_____

The trait of serving should still be passed down to disciples today. Needs should still be getting met. Clearly, a disciple is supposed to be a minister.

MEMORY VERSE

Mark 10:45

WEEKLY BIBLE READING

Read the passage and write out an insight on at least one of the following:

A: Attitude to change
C: Command to obey
T: Truth to believe
S: Sin to confess

☐ **MONDAY**
John 13:12-20

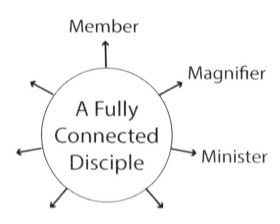

19

A DISCIPLE MEETS
NEEDS AND SERVES OTHERS

WEEKLY BIBLE READING

❑ **TUESDAY**
Romans 12:6-8

If you ask the typical church person how many "ministers" they have in their church, they will most likely tell you the number of pastors they have on their pastoral staff. What that person fails to realize is that every disciple in the church is actually a "minister" for Christ. Everyone is not called to be a paid pastor, but everyone is called to be a "minister" for Jesus Christ.

A minister is simply someone that meets the need of another person. A minister is simply a servant. In John 13:1-19 Jesus emphasizes the importance of every disciple being a servant or minister by washing the feet of His disciples. In John 13:15 Jesus said, *"For I have given you an example, that you also should do just as I have done to you."*

In this passage Jesus is stressing the priority of every single disciple learning how to serve one another. In the book of Acts, we see the church in Jerusalem filled with servants. In Acts 4:34 the scripture says, *"There was not a needy person among them."* Clearly the church is designed to be a place where disciples of Christ live lifestyles of service. Imagine what it would be like if every person in your local church was committed to serving like Jesus served?

❑ **WEDNESDAY**
Luke 10:25-37

Sadly, the church is filled with plenty of people who never serve. In fact, there are some people who spend their entire lives calling themselves Christ followers and never minister to anyone. That is a contradiction in terms. A Christ follower is a servant!

The church must be a place where we help people discover their role as a servant. The church should be an environment where a person can use their spiritual gift, talents, personality, and abilities to meet the needs of others.

The church ought to be an army of servants. In an army every soldier has a role and a responsibility. When mobilized, those soldiers become a force to be reckoned with. What if the church were a force to be reckoned with? She could be that force if every disciple knew their role and responsibility. When every disciple is a minister, the enemy better be on the look out!

Where do you serve in the context of a local church?

_____

_____

❒ **THURSDAY**
Mark 10:35-45

WHAT DOES MINISTRY MEAN?

Ministry can happen in two different ways for every disciple. There is informal ministry, and there is formal ministry. You could also call it individual and spontaneous ministry or team and planned ministry. Here is the difference. An example of formal ministry might be something like serving in the worship ministry or hospitality ministry of your church. There are many more examples of formal ministry roles. An example of spontaneous ministry would be cooking a meal for someone in your small group or church. There are obviously many examples of serving in a spontaneous manner.

❒ **FRIDAY**
Acts 6:1-7

The point that needs to be made here is that a disciple serves in both formal and informal types of ministry. A disciple looks for a place of ministry in his or her church as well as watching for random needs that can be met at any place and any time. Simply put, disciples look for ways to meet the needs of others because that's what Jesus did!

If you have a desire to minister and serve the way Jesus did, there are two things to consider. First, know your spiritual gift. God gives spiritual gifts to every believer to empower the way they serve. What spiritual gifts does Paul mention in Romans 12:6-8? _____

_____

_____

When you are meeting needs in the area of your giftedness, you will be energized and see fruit from your ministry.

A second thing to consider is that meeting needs happens best within the body of Christ. Since God has gifted everyone differently, it stands to reason that we need each other. If everyone is working together with their spiritual gifts, a lot of needs will be met. What does Peter say in 1 Peter 4:10?_____

_____

When a church is filled with people using the gifts God has given them, many needs will be met. The point is simple. Discover your gift and use it in the context of a church body!

There will be times when a need exists that must to be met regardless of your giftedness and regardless of whether or not you are in a church. Sometimes you simply see a need and fill it!

WHAT HAPPENED TO MINISTRY?

One of the worst things that ever happened to ministry might well have been the day ministry became a vocation. In other words, once people started getting paid to do ministry, some people stopped doing ministry all together. Don't misunderstand. There is nothing wrong with vocational ministry, unless it causes us to forget that every believer is a minister!

At the beginning of this lesson, we talked about how many ministers you have in your church. The number of ministers in your church ought to equal the total number of members you have in your church. Every disciple is a minister.

Imagine what would happen in our world if every disciple were a minister? If every disciple was serving and meeting needs, the world would be a different place. Perhaps this is exactly why Jesus told us to make disciples of "all nations." By making disciples of "all nations," we are literally placing servants all over the world!

QUESTIONS FOR GROUP DISCUSSION OR PERSONAL REFLECTION

➤ Open your group with prayer and share an example of how you've been able to serve someone recently.

➤ When you hear the word "servant," who is the first person that comes to your mind and why?

➤ Read John 13:14 and Acts 4:34. Is there a connection in these verses? Explain.

➤ Read Mark 10:45. Do you agree or disagree that a non-serving Christian is a contradiction?

➤ Explain the difference between formal and informal ministry. How does a person participate in both types of service?

➤ Read Romans 12:6-8. What is your spiritual gift and how have you used it in ministry?

➤ What happens when the body of Christ is not utilizing the gifts God has given? What happens when it is?

➤ What ministry role do you currently serve in within a local church context?

➤ How does the church encourage and assist more people to find their place of service?

➤ Take a minute to share prayer concerns and pray together.

WEEK FIVE:
A DISCIPLE IS MATURING

Goal: To understand the trait of maturity.

No one would argue that the disciples that followed Jesus were significantly more spiritually mature after having spent time with Jesus than they were prior to doing so. One could argue that there are plenty of Christians today who have been in the church for many years that don't seem any more mature spiritually than when they were first saved. Something is wrong with that picture!

The longer a person has been a believer, the more spiritual maturity should be demonstrated in their life. Not only was this true of Jesus' original disciples, it was also true of their disciples. Believers in the Jerusalem church were becoming more spiritually mature over time. How does Acts 5:28 indicate the spiritual growth of believers in the Jerusalem church? _____

_____

_____

It is clear that being a disciple means experiencing spiritual maturity.

MEMORY VERSE

John 8:31

WEEKLY BIBLE READING

Read the passage and write out an insight on at least one of the following:

A: Attitude to change
C: Command to obey
T: Truth to believe
S: Sin to confess

☐ **MONDAY**
Hebrews 5:11-6:2

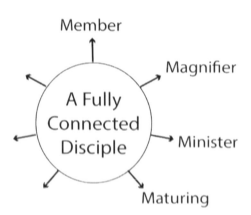

If I know one thing about Christ's disciples, it would be this. They experienced significant spiritual maturity over the few short years they walked with Jesus. So much so, Jesus was able to put the reins of His movement in their hands with just three years of training. In John 20:21 Jesus said, *"As the Father has sent me, even so I am sending you."*

The observation mentioned above leads to an important question. Are the disciples in our churches today experiencing enough spiritual growth in a few years that they could lead the church into the near future? In case you are still pondering that question the answer is, "not hardly"!

I think it is safe to say that in many churches it takes years for spiritual infants to become spiritual children and even longer to become spiritual adolescents. The idea of developing spiritual adults just isn't a reality in a vast majority of churches. Is it any wonder why the church isn't pushing back more of the darkness when many of her leaders are still walking around in spiritual diapers?

Something has to change! The expectation in the church today has to become one of spiritual growth. Seeing people move from infancy to adulthood has to be the norm rather than the exception!

The church must regain her focus of helping totally disconnected people become fully connected disciples by helping people connect to an intentional process of spiritual development. This intentional process must be designed to help people move from spiritual infancy to spiritual adulthood. The future of the church is riding on this priority!

A number of churches have become places where

people are jumping from one study course to another. They watch one DVD study and then go to the next "latest and greatest" best selling Bible study. Whatever happened to learning the basics of the faith and then intentionally moving to a deeper understanding of the scriptures and theology? I wonder how Paul's words in Colossians 2:7, *"rooted and built up in him and established in the faith,"* would stack up with the current state of discipleship in the Church today?

☐ **THURSDAY**
Acts 9:17-25

We must return to the priority of helping every disciple grow to maturity in the faith. We must be intentional about spiritual growth.

WHAT DOES MATURITY MEAN?

Maturity means growth. It means being in the process of becoming more like Jesus. When a person comes to faith in Christ, they are a spiritual newborn. As they grow, they mature into a spiritual child, adolescent, and then into a spiritual adult. The Apostle John makes these stages of spiritual growth and maturity very clear in 1 John 2:12-14. What are some the marks of maturity you see in this passage? _____

☐ **FRIDAY**
Colossians 2:1-7

_____

_____

_____

_____

Moving from spiritual infancy to spiritual adulthood does not happen overnight. Spiritual maturity takes time. It is the by-product of at least two ingredients: knowledge and experience. Maturity is not just the result of increased knowledge or increased experience. It is a result of both! When a person's knowledge and experience with God increases over time, maturity results.

One passage that speaks clearly to the priority of spiritual maturity is found in Hebrews 5:11-14. What was the problem explained in this passage? _____

_____

_____

What is needed when a person is a spiritual infant?__

_____

What is needed when a person is more mature in their faith? _____

What does Hebrews 6:1 encourage believers to do? _

_____

_____

The goal for every believer is maturity. Disciples are supposed to be growing!

WHAT HAPPENED TO DISCIPLESHIP?

Jesus came to start a movement to accomplish His mission. In order to leave His mission and movement in the hands of competent leaders, they had to be developed. The individuals He chose to be His leaders had to have a spiritual birth and spiritual growth before they would ever be in the position to lead the movement. Jesus accomplished this through discipleship. He took a handful of ordinary and uneducated men and He gave them the knowledge and experience they needed to be mature enough to lead His movement. How does Mark 3:14 describe what Jesus did? _____

_____

_____

By spending time with Jesus and being taught by Him, the disciples grew into spiritually mature leaders. This is the same process the church needs today!

The next generation will not be able to keep the mission and movement of Christ going unless we are developing spiritually mature disciples that can lead. This is why the church desperately needs to be making disciples that make disciples. If we do not make disciples the way Jesus did, the whole movement of Christianity will come to a screeching halt.

Every believer should be a part of a discipleship process that helps them connect to a small group where they can become more like Jesus. They need to connect to a growth environment where they move from infancy to adulthood. This environment needs to have a balance of both knowledge and experience. It should begin with the basics of the faith and lead to deeper truths of scripture. What was said of the ordinary and uneducated disciples in Acts 4:13?_____

_____

_____

QUESTIONS FOR GROUP DISCUSSION OR PERSONAL REFLECTION

- Open your group with prayer and share someone you are trying to reach out to for Christ.

- Describe some area of your life where you have grown in knowledge and experience besides your faith.

- How would you describe the growth journey of your spiritual life?

- Read 1 John 2:12-14. Which stage of spiritual development do you see yourself in currently? Why?

- Give some examples of how the original disciples matured spiritually.

- Describe what the discipleship process might have looked like with Jesus and His disciples.

- Describe some of the times when you feel like you have grown the most spiritually?

- Read 2 Timothy 3:16-17. What role does knowledge play in the spiritual growth process?

- Read 1 Corinthians 3:1-3. How does our character and conduct demonstrate our level of spiritual maturity?

- Take a minute to share prayer concerns and pray together.

WEEK SIX:
A DISCIPLE IS A MANAGER

Goal: To understand the trait of managing.

The original disciples never took a money management course, but they learned from the Master how to honor God with their resources. The original disciples never attended a time management workshop, but they learned from the Master how to live by the right priorities. The original disciples never went to a healthy living class, but they learned from the Master how to honor God with their bodies. The disciples of Jesus learned how to manage their lives in a way that honored God the Father by watching how Jesus managed His life!

A disciple that lives like Jesus is a disciple that is becoming a good manager.

MEMORY VERSE

Acts 2:45

WEEKLY BIBLE READING

Read the passage and write out an insight on at least one of the following:

A: Attitude to change
C: Command to obey
T: Truth to believe
S: Sin to confess

☐ **MONDAY**
Acts 4:32-37

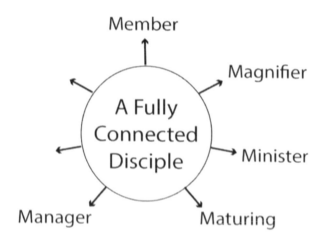

A DISCIPLE HONORS GOD WITH RESOURCES

WEEKLY BIBLE READING

_____

◻ **TUESDAY**
Acts 5:1-11

I have a pretty strong hunch that the disciples managed their resources drastically different after spending three years with Jesus than they did before they met Him. In fact, I would even suggest that the disciples weren't really that concerned with how they managed their resources until Jesus gave them a new purpose for their lives.

I am also convinced that the disciples in the church in Jerusalem understood the importance of honoring God with their resources as well. In Acts 2:45 the Bible says, *"And they were selling their possessions and belongings and distributing the proceeds to all, as any had need."*

The New Testament disciples were sharing their resources because of the influence Christ had on His disciples. As the Lord taught the original disciples how to be managers of their resources, they taught their disciples how to be managers of their resources. They were actually multiplying managers as they multiplied disciples!

◻ **WEDNESDAY**
Matthew
6:19-24

Even today the end product of being a disciple ought to include being a better manager. The longer you walk with and learn from Jesus, the more concerned you should be with how you manage your time, treasure, temple, and talents. Being with Jesus changes how you manage your time, money, body, and abilities.

If you have been a disciple for very long and you do not look at your life resources differently, you have missed an important part of what it means to become more like Jesus. Jesus clearly managed His earthly resources in a way that honored the Father and expanded the kingdom.

So how are you managing your resources of time, treasure, talent, and temple? Have you grown in the way you manage your God given resources since you started following Christ? Have you come to the place where you realize that all you have actually belongs to God and all that matters is how you manage it? Are you a disciple that manages your resources to further the kingdom of God? A fully developed disciple is a manager of their God-given resources!

WHAT DOES MANAGING MEAN?

There is quite a difference between ownership and management. A manager simply takes care of what belongs to the owner. A manager is often called a steward. A steward is someone who looks after the property of someone else. Since God owns everything we have, we are stewards of our God-given resources. A disciple takes care of God's property.

☐ **THURSDAY**
Matthew
25:14-30

In the life of every disciple, there are four things that belong to God. God has entrusted into your care your time, treasure, temple, and talent. Let's walk through each of these God-given resources.

Time! Time is a God-given resource to be used for His glory. Time is a gift that God entrusts to each disciple to be managed in a way that honors Him. Every disciple can choose to maximize the time God has given him or her or to waste it. What did Jesus do with His time according to John 17:4?_____

☐ **FRIDAY**
Mark 12:41-44

_____

_____

Jesus used His time wisely, and He completed the work that His Father had given Him to do.

Treasure! Treasure simply means money or possessions. All the stuff you have belongs to God. What does Psalm 24:1 tell you? _____

_____

_____

The earth and everything in it belongs to God. All you have is simply on loan to you for a short time. What you do with what you have been given matters a great

The earth and everything in it belongs to God. All you have is simply on loan to you for a short time. What you do with what you have been given matters a great deal to God. If you use the treasure God has given you to honor Him, you will please the Lord. If you waste it, you will dishonor the Lord. What principle did Jesus teach in the parable of the talents in Matthew 25:14-30?

_____

_____

Temple! Your body is the temple of the Holy Spirit. So how you manage it is extremely important. What does Paul say in 1 Corinthians 6:19? _____

_____

_____

Since your body is the temple of the Holy Spirit, you should want to do your best to keep your body healthy and holy. This means taking care of your body and avoiding things that might harm your body. Managing your body well allows you to maximize the time you have to build the kingdom of God.

Talent! One of the resources God gives everyone is a talent, gift, or ability that can be used for Him. Imagine what would happen if everyone in the church managed their God-given talent, gift, or ability to build the kingdom of God and serve others. A church that was mobilized with good stewards would be a church that is making a serious dent in the darkness of this world. What does 1 Peter 4:10 say? _____

_____

_____

WHAT HAPPENED TO MANAGING?

Somehow in the past two thousand years, the idea that a disciple is a manager has become very blurry. We have lost sight of the truth that being a disciple means using the resources that God has given us in ways that honor Him. This concept, however, was very clear in the New Testament church. The early disciples were known for using what God had given them to care for one another. In fact, very early in the life of the church, God made an example of two people, Ananias and Sapphira, who did not honor God with their treasure. What happened to Ananias and Sapphira in Acts 5:1-11? _____

_____

_____

Don't make the same mistake Ananias and Sapphira made. Honor God with the resources He has blessed you with!

QUESTIONS FOR GROUP DISCUSSION OR PERSONAL REFLECTION

➤ Open your group with prayer and share an example of how you've shared your faith or invited someone to church recently.

➤ When you hear the word "steward," what is your first thought?

➤ In what ways do think Jesus modeled stewardship or management for His original disciples?

➤ Read Acts 2:44-45 and Acts 4:34-37 and explain how managing was evident in the Jerusalem church.

➤ Read Acts 5:1-5. Why do you think God allowed Ananias to die?

➤ Which of the following — time, treasure, temple, or talent —are you managing well and which needs improvement?

➤ What are the benefits of managing well and the drawbacks of not managing well?

➤ Why do you think people struggle so much today with managing the resources God has given them?

➤ What are some keys you've discovered to managing your resources better?

➤ Take a minute to share prayer concerns and pray together.

WEEK SEVEN:
A DISCIPLE IS A MESSENGER

Goal: To understand the trait of being a messenger.

One of the very first things Jesus called His disciples was "fishers of men." He was making a point from the very beginning that He intended for them to be messengers of the gospel. During the years Jesus spent with those disciples, He modeled and He taught the importance of sharing the message of salvation with everyone that needed to hear it. When Jesus made disciples, He was clearly making messengers!

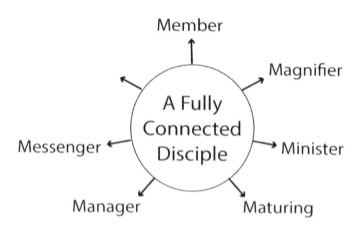

MEMORY VERSE

Luke 19:10

WEEKLY BIBLE READING

Read the passage and write out an insight on at least one of the following:

A: Attitude to change
C: Command to obey
T: Truth to believe
S: Sin to confess

☐ **MONDAY**
Matthew 4:18-25

A DISCIPLE CARES AND SHARES

Every disciple that has lived during the past two thousand years should bear the mark of a "messenger for Christ." Every disciple is called to share the message of Jesus Christ. The "good news" is supposed to be shared!

In Acts 5:42 the Bible says, *"And every day, in the temple and from house to house, they did not cease teaching and preaching that Christ is Jesus."* The disciples did not stop talking about Jesus because they knew they were Christ's messengers. Spreading the news about Jesus was not an option for New Testament disciples.

**WEEKLY BIBLE
READING**

☐ **TUESDAY**
Luke 19:1-10

Spreading the good news about Jesus should not be an option for disciples today. It should be a part of our everyday activity. Since we know that people who are far from God need salvation, we should be committed to sharing the gospel with everyone we possibly can. Jesus modeled this priority in His life. His coming, in itself, is an example of being a messenger. Jesus came to earth to communicate God's love and forgiveness to fallen man. Jesus also gives us many practical examples of how He lived His life as a messenger. One of those examples found in John chapter four was an encounter Jesus had with a woman at a well. After Jesus shared the message of salvation with this woman, His disciples were wondering why He was talking to her. In John 4:34 Jesus told His disciples, *"My food is to do the will of him who sent me and to accomplish his work."*

☐ **WEDNESDAY**
Matthew
5:13-16

In this same passage Jesus told His disciples that He was sending them to be laborers in the harvest. That meant He was sending them to be messengers in the same way that He was a messenger. Jesus expected His disciples to be messengers and He expected their disciples to be messengers! The disciples were actually multiplying messengers as they multiplied disciples.

So here is a great question. When was the last time you shared the message of Jesus with someone? When was the last time you cared about someone's spiritual condition enough that you were willing to ask that person if they knew Jesus? If you can't remember the last time you shared the message of Christ, you might not be a true messenger.

WHAT DOES MESSENGER MEAN?

One of the ways Jesus describes disciples as messengers is by calling them "light." A world filled with spiritual darkness certainly needs people who can shine for Christ. Read Matthew 5:14-16 and write down a truth or two from what Jesus says about being the light of the world. _____

_____

_____

As you think about being light in a dark world, let's use the letters of the word *"light"* to help you become a better messenger.

☐ **THURSDAY**
Acts 5:33-42

Look! The first step in being a better messenger is to look for opportunities to share the message of salvation. What did Jesus tell His disciples to do in John 4:35? _____

_____

_____

Jesus told His disciples that the harvest was ripe. If they would open their eyes and "look," they could see the many opportunities they had to share the message of salvation.

Initiate connections! The second step in being a better messenger is to connect with the opportunities you see. Being a better messenger is about building relationships with people who are far from God. What did Philip do according to Acts 8:30? _____

☐ **FRIDAY**
Romans 10:14-21

_____

Philip was prompted by the Holy Spirit to initiate a connection so he could share with the Ethiopian. God is still in the business of calling us to initiate connections with people.

Go to God in prayer! We need to be praying for God to work in the lives of the people we have connected with. This might be a prayer in your mind while talking with someone or it might be ongoing prayer for someone. What was Paul's prayer according to Romans 10:1? _____

_____

_____

What was Paul concerned with in Colossians 4:3,4? _

_____

_____

_____

_____

_____

_____

_____

_____

_____

_____

_____

_____

_____

_____

_____

_____

_____

_____

_____

_____

Paul was asking the Colossians to pray that he would have open doors to share the message of Christ.

Help people in tangible ways! Helping people in a time of need is a great way to build a relationship and show love to those you want to share Christ with. Acts of kindness toward someone can open doors that words can't. What does Romans 2:4 say about the kindness of God? _____

_____

_____

There are always people in our lives that have physical, emotional, social, and spiritual needs which God can use us to help meet. Helping to meet those needs can help pave the way for the message of Christ to be received.

Tell people the message of Jesus! The ultimate goal of being a messenger is to say something. Actions can speak, but sooner or later the goal is to communicate the message of salvation with our words. What does Romans 10:14 say about preaching? _____

_____

_____

Just remember that someone spoke to you about Jesus at some point in your life. You heard the message because someone loved you enough to share it with you. Who in your life needs to hear the message of Jesus? ___

_____

_____

Always remember to be light...

>**L:** Look for opportunities
>**I:** Initiate connections with people
>**G:** God to God in prayer
>**H:** Help people in tangible ways
>**T:** Tell people the message of Jesus

QUESTIONS FOR GROUP DISCUSSION
OR PERSONAL REFLECTION

➤ Open your group with prayer and share a highlight from your week.

➤ When you think of a "messenger" for Christ, who comes to your mind?

➤ When you think of your own life, how effective of a messenger are you?

➤ Read Acts 5:42. How would describe the mark of a messenger among the disciples in the Jerusalem church?

➤ Why is it difficult for some disciples to be messengers of the good news?

➤ Where do you find opportunities to connect with lost people?

➤ What should motivate us to be better messengers for Christ?

➤ Why should prayer be an integral part of personal evangelism?

➤ Read Romans 2:4. What are some practical ways you can show people kindness that leads to repentance?

➤ Who are some people in your life right now that need to hear the message of Jesus?

➤ Take a minute and pray for the people you need to share Christ with.

WEEK EIGHT:
A DISCIPLE IS A MULTIPLIER

Goal: To understand the trait of multiplication.

Jesus came to do two important things. He came to redeem mankind, and He came to start a movement of redemption. When a person is redeemed, they are able to become a disciple of Jesus Christ. When a person becomes a disciple of Jesus Christ, they should have a desire to see others be a part of this movement of redemption.

This movement of redemption was started in order to reach every person, in every nation, throughout every generation, by disciples that are multipliers. Sadly, most disciples never multiply one single disciple. That was never God's plan. Jesus made disciples that would in turn multiply even more disciples. Through multiplication the message of redemption could be spread to the entire world in a very short period of time. Every disciple ought to be a multiplier!

MEMORY VERSE

2 Timothy 2:2

WEEKLY BIBLE READING

Read the passage and write out an insight on at least one of the following:

A: Attitude to change
C: Command to obey
T: Truth to believe
S: Sin to confess

☐ **MONDAY**
2 Timothy
2:1-13

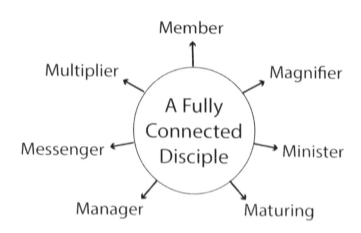

A DISCIPLE MAKES AND MULTIPLIES DISCIPLES

When Jesus gathered His disciples together on a mountainside to give them the Great Commission, which ones did He really expect to make disciples? If you answered "all of them," you answered correctly!

Jesus gave the commission to "make disciples" to all of His disciples. He wasn't expecting only a few of them to make disciples; He was expecting all of them to do so. This is really the only way we can reach "all nations."

I have met so many people that live like the commission to make disciples is optional. Many people think that Jesus was only expecting those with certain gifts, abilities, or training to make disciples. Not so! Jesus was expecting ordinary, average people to obey His command to make more disciples.

An ordinary, average person means you! Jesus expects you to multiply more disciples. This can happen when you make a disciple that turns around and makes more disciples. If you repeat this process effectively and consistently, you will leave behind thousands of disciples and a legacy that keeps growing when you are gone.

Every single disciple is called to multiply more disciples. In John 20:21 Jesus said, *"As the Father has sent me, even so I am sending you."* Jesus expected His disciples to be marked by a lifestyle of multiplication. He expected His disciples to do the same thing He had done with them. Sadly, there are very few Christians that are living as multipliers today. You would probably have a hard time identifying a handful of disciples that have more than one generation of disciples that are a product of their intentional influence.

Why are so few Christians multiplying more disciples? I believe the enemy attacks a commitment to a life of multiplication more than anything else in this world. Why? Because multiplication is where the power is! The enemy will even concede movements of addition as long as there is no possibility of a movement of multiplication. Satan will always attack the potential for exponential growth.

☐ **THURSDAY**
John 20:19-23

WHAT DOES MULTIPLYING MEAN?

If one person was able to reach one other person for Christ each week for the next sixteen years, he would reach a total of 936 people. If a person reached one person for Christ every day, he would reach 5,840 in sixteen years.

If, however, a person reached one person for Christ in six months and then both of you reach one more person in the next six months, then four people will be reached. If that process continues of people who are reached helping reach more people, a movement of multiplication will begin that in sixteen years will total over 4 billion people!

☐ **FRIDAY**
Acts 1:1-11

1 year	=	4	/ 1.5 years	=	8
2 years	=	16	/ 2.5 years	=	32
3 years	=	64	/ 3.5 years	=	128
4 years	=	256	/ 4.5 years	=	512
5 years	=	1024	/ 5.5 years	=	2048
6 years	=	4096	/ 6.5 years	=	8192
16 years	=	4,294,961,26 people!			

I guess now we know why Jesus said make disciples of all nations!

In John 15:8 Jesus states very clearly one of the signs that proves a person is a disciple. What does Jesus say?___

_____

_____

Having a "much fruit" life does not happen by accident. Bearing much fruit is the result of intentional investing in the lives of disciples that will in turn invest in other disciples. If your goal is to bear "much fruit," consider the following.

Focus on a few! Jesus started a movement of multiplication by focusing on a small group not a large crowd. Jesus invested His life deeper in a few so that He could eventually go wider. How many men did Jesus focus on according to Mark 3:14? _____

_____

_____

Recruit reliable people! Jesus did not pick the most gifted or most educated, but He did select "reliable" men. Jesus chose men that were willing to count the cost to follow Him. What did Jesus say in Matthew 16:24? _____

_____

_____

Unified plan! Jesus gave His disciples principles that could be passed down through multiple generations of disciples. What were these principles called in Acts 2:42?

_____

_____

Jesus did not teach His disciples everything they could know, but He did teach them the things they needed to know.

Intentional process! Jesus was very intentional about the way He went about making disciples. He gave them a perfect balance of both information and application. Jesus taught His disciples and He modeled for His disciples exactly what He wanted them to be and do. What two words describe Jesus' process in Mark 3:14? __

_____

_____

Target clearly defined! The end product of being one of Christ's disciples was very clearly defined, in Matthew 28:19 "make disciples." The target for the disciples of Jesus was not to make more worshippers, more Bible students, or deeper fellowship. The target was to reproduce disciples that live and lead like Jesus. What did John say in 1 John 2:6? _____

_____

_____

If you will spend the next year investing in a disciple that will turn around and do the same thing with another disciple while you do the same thing, you will soon be multiplying disciples. Very few people do this, so be one of the few.

QUESTIONS FOR GROUP DISCUSSION
OR PERSONAL REFLECTION

➤ Open your group with prayer and share something God has been teaching you recently.

➤ Can you give some examples of multiplying movements besides the Church? Why do you think they succeeded?

➤ Read Matthew 28:19-20. Why do you think there are so few multiplying disciples today? How many multipliers do you know personally?

➤ Why is God's plan a movement of multiplication rather than a movement of addition? How does Satan attack a movement of multiplication?

➤ Read Mark 3:14. What was Christ's approach to make multiplying disciples? Read 2 Timothy 2:2. How is Paul's approach similar to Christ's?

➤ Do you think the Church can be a movement of multiplication? What would it take to see that become a reality?

➤ What has been your own personal experience with disciple making?

➤ Have you multiplied any disciples?

➤ Take a minute and share prayer requests and pray together.

A FEW FINAL THOUGHTS...

Congratulations! You have finished *Discipleship Essentials*. Hopefully you have applied yourself wholeheartedly to this study and are growing as a disciple of Christ.

Now you know some of the essential marks of a disciple of Jesus. If you continue to develop these traits in your life, you will grow closer to God, become more like Christ, and find your place in His church.

It is time now to take your next step as a disciple and work through another course in the Disciple Making Essentials Series. You may also want to check out more resources from Impact Ministries. Check out the Impact Ministries page in the back of this book or look us up on the web at impactdisciples. com.

KEEP GROWING AS A DISCIPLE OF CHRIST!

Inspiring People and Churches to Be
and Build Disciples of Jesus Christ

EXPLORE

We invite you to EXPLORE and DISCOVER the concepts of
DISCIPLE MAKING by checking out the following RESOURCES.

◆The Impact Blog ◆The Impact Newsletter
◆The Impact Audio and Video Podcasts

EDUCATE

We encourage you to LEARN more about DISCIPLE MAKING
through our written RESOURCES and TRAINING opportunities.

◆The DMC Training ◆315 Leadership Training ◆Free Resources

ESTABLISH

We seek to HELP you start a DISCIPLE MAKING MOVEMENT
by showing you how to LAUNCH a disciple making group.

◆The Impact Weekend ◆The Essentials ◆Vision Consultation

ENGAGE

We invite you to JOIN with Impact Ministries in spreading the
VISION of DISCIPLE MAKING around the WORLD through
several involvement opportunities.

◆Join our Prayer Team ◆Be an Impact Trainer ◆Partner with Us

CONTACT US

◆ImpactDisciples.com ◆Info@ImpactDisciples.com ◆678.854.9322

Made in the USA
Columbia, SC
27 February 2019